FOR
BOB & JAN

Timothy R. Botts

1994

S E V E N T Y - F I V E

P R O V E R B S

F R O M

The Living Bible

· ·

CALLIGRAPHIC ILLUSTRATION AND

Tyndale House Publishers, Inc.
WHEATON, ILLINOIS

PROVERBS

RAYERS BY *Timothy R. Botts*

Published in association with the literary agency of Alive
Communications, P.O. Box 49068, Colorado Springs, CO 80949.

Library of Congress Cataloging-in-Publication Data
Bible. O.T. Proverbs. English. Living Bible. Selections. 1994.
   Proverbs : 75 proverbs from the Living Bible / calligraphic
 illustration and prayers by Timothy R. Botts.
     p. cm.
   Includes index.
   ISBN 0-8423-5034-9
   I. Botts, Timothy R. II. Title.
  BS1463.B68 1994
  223'.705208—dc20   94-12127

Printed in Mexico

99 98 97 96 95 94
6 5 4 3 2

· · ·

To Dad Botts and Dad Bonner

    for your steadfast example and

To Nancy

    "There are many fine women in the world,

    but you are the best of them all."

PROVERBS 31:29

THE BIBLICAL BOOK OF PROVERBS contains the wisdom that has been the basis of Judeo-Christian culture for millennia. My interest as an artist is to make a contemporary expression of these great words through the vivid language of *The Living Bible* along with my expressive style of calligraphy.

I have stretched myself artistically by adding illustrated initials throughout to symbolize the book's many themes. These proverbs are chosen from more than nine hundred and relate to life at home, at work, in government, and fundamentally with God. Their humor, frankness, and relevance to our time is startling.

I have established a daily discipline of entering verses into a sketchbook diary along with prayer responses. These are included to help you meditate on these nuggets of truth. It brings me great joy to present this book to you because it offers the secrets of living life in perfect balance.

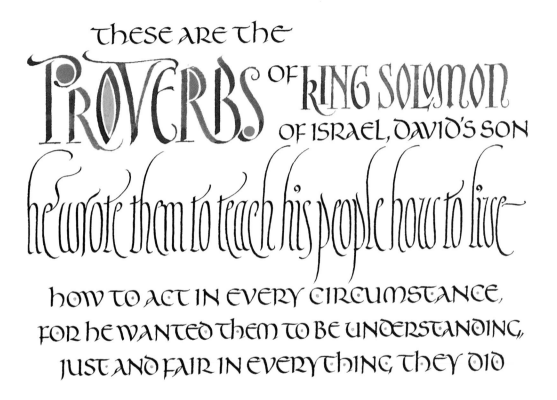

these are the
PROVERBS OF KING SOLOMON
OF ISRAEL, DAVID'S SON
he wrote them to teach his people how to live—
HOW TO ACT IN EVERY CIRCUMSTANCE,
FOR HE WANTED THEM TO BE UNDERSTANDING,
JUST AND FAIR IN EVERYTHING THEY DID

PROVERBS 1 : 1 - 3

OUR LORD,
as creator of
all things,
I acknowledge
you as the source
of all wisdom.
I humble myself
before you,
ready to learn.

But all who listen to me shall live in peace and safety unafraid

PROVERBS 1:33

GRACIOUS God,
thank you for
having our best
interests in mind.
Before my work,
my family,
my money,
I will put you
first.

In everything you do
PUT GOD FIRST
and he will direct you
and crown your efforts
with success

PROVERBS 3:6

LORD of abundance and excellence, help me not to forget the source of all that I have. Help me to be as generous as you are.

HONOR THE LORD

by giving him the first part
of all your income,
and he will fill your barns
with wheat and barley
and overflow your wine vats
with the finest wines. PROVERBS 3:9-10

*TO the God of
perfect balance,
help me not
to go beyond
appreciation
and enjoyment
of those things
that could
sidetrack me
from your
purposes for
my life.
Help me to
remember that
I am responsible
for the choices
I make.*

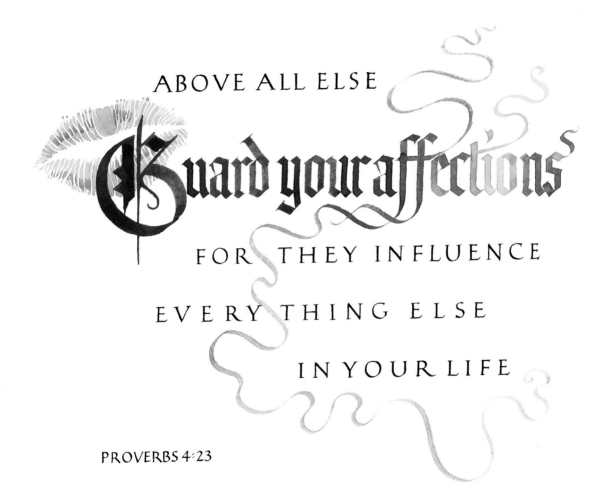

ABOVE ALL ELSE

Guard your affections

FOR THEY INFLUENCE

EVERY THING ELSE

IN YOUR LIFE

PROVERBS 4:23

*CREATOR of
male and female,
help us to enjoy
each other as
much as you
intended. Help us
to take the time
and have the
sensitivity
to satisfy
each other's
needs.*

ET YOUR
MANHOOD
BE A BLESSING,

Rejoice in the wife of your youth.
Let her charms and tender embrace
satisfy you,
Let her love alone fill you
with delight.

PROVERBS 5:18-19

*HOLY GOD,
forgive me. Help
me to have a
healthy view of
myself, live by
the truth, actively
love difficult
people, be a
helper and a
builder, do the
right thing,
be accurate with
my words, and
contribute to
peace.*

THERE
ARE SIX
THINGS
THE
LORD
HATES-
NO,
SEVEN:

HAUGHTINESS
LYING
MURDERING
plotting evil
EAGERNESS TO DO WRONG
A FALSE WITNESS
SOWING DISCORD
AMONG BROTHERS

PROVERBS 6:16-19

*HEAVENLY
Father, thank you
for parents who
cared for me
when I was
helpless.
Show me how
to honor them
in appreciation.
Help me to
remember that
their experience
always exceeds
my own.*

BEY YOUR FATHER
AND YOUR MOTHER
for their advice is a beam of light
directed into the dark corners of
your mind to warn you of danger
and to give you a good life.

PROVERBS 6:20,23

LORD OF LIFE,
forgive me for
procrastinating.
Help me to
remember that
opportunities are
limited.
Help me to get
going!

A wise youth makes hay while the sun shines but what a shame to see a lad who sleeps away his hour of opportunity.

PROVERBS 10:5

*GOD of peace,
help me to learn
the power of
silence.*

WISE PEOPLE HOLD THEIR TONGUE

Only fools blurt out everything they know;
That only leads to sorrow and trouble.

PROVERBS 10:14

RIGHTEOUS
God, help me
remember how
unfair it is to be
paid for doing
nothing. Help me
to hold up my
end of the
bargain.

lazy fellow is a pain
to his employers—
like smoke in their eyes
or vinegar that sets the teeth on edge.

PROVERBS 10:26

ETERNAL Father, thank you for helping me to face my own death. My only hope is in you. How I thank you for the promise of heaven beyond.

WHEN EVIL PEOPLE DIE, THEIR HOPES ALL PERISH FOR THEY ARE BASED UPON THIS EARTHLY LIFE

PROVERBS 11:7

LORD of the city,
I can make a
difference!
Help me to
take a stand
against evil by
contributing
positively
to enrich and
rebuild
our culture.

The good influence of godly citizens
causes a city to prosper
but the moral decay of the wicked
drives it downhill

PROVERBS 11:11

LORD of the big picture, help me to see the difference between winning the lottery and gaining a place in heaven!

The evil person gets rich for the moment

BUT THE GOOD PERSON'S REWARD
LASTS F O R E V E R

PROVERBS 11:18

*LORD OF ALL
beauty, thank you
for creating us
male and female.
Help us not to
flaunt what is a
gift. Help us to
enhance and not
detract from
your gift.*

A BEAUTIFUL WOMAN
lacking discretion & modesty
is like a fine gold ring
in a pig's snout

PROVERBS 11:22

*MOST
bountiful God,
your system is
just the opposite
of ours on earth.
Free me from
my prison of
selfishness.
Give me a
big and open
heart toward
the needs
around me.*

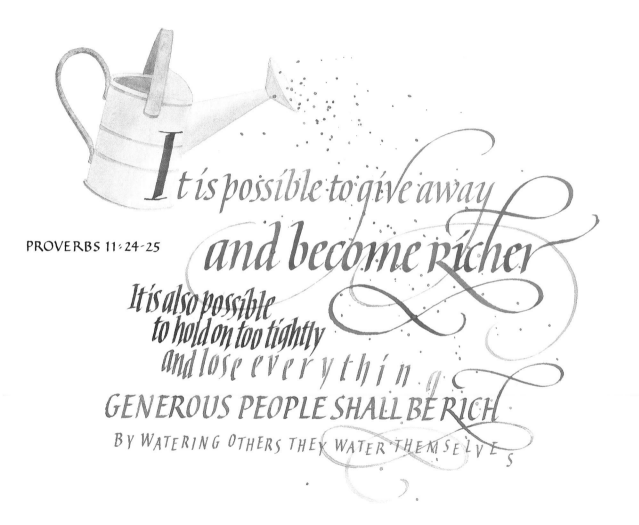

PROVERBS 11·24-25

It is possible to give away and become richer It is also possible to hold on too tightly and lose everything GENEROUS PEOPLE SHALL BE RICH BY WATERING OTHERS THEY WATER THEMSELVES

*SUSTAINER of
all life, forgive
me for focusing
on money
instead of you.
Thank you for
this beautiful
metaphor of
strength. Help me
to remain
connected to you.*

Trust in your money
and down you go

TRUST IN GOD
and flourish as a tree

PROVERBS 11:28

LORD of even dust and mud, help me to contribute to the economy and not be part of the problem. It is good to clean the toilet and take out the trash!

I
t is better to
get your hands dirty
and eat
than to be TOO PROUD TO WORK
and starve

PROVERBS 12:9

*CREATOR God,
thank you for the
fascination and
companionship
you provide for
us through the
animal kingdom.
Help us not to
misuse our power
over them.*

GOOD PEOPLE
are concerned
for the welfare of
their animals

PROVERBS 12:10

but even the kindness of
godless people is cruel.

LORD
of generosity,
help me to learn
the contentment
and peace of
mind that comes
from being a
giver.

Crooks are jealous of each other's loot while good people long to help each other.

PROVERBS 12:12

*FAITHFUL God,
help me to think
hard before
promising and
then to be
someone
people can count
on. Thank you,
also, that joy is
part of your
nature.*

GOD delights in those who keep their promises.

PROVERBS 12:22

LORD,
to whom the
earth belongs,
you knew all
about recycling
before we ever
thought of it!
Forgive me for
my carelessness.
Help me to
exercise
creativity with
all stuff.

DILIGENT PEOPLE make good use of EVERYTHING they find.

PROVERBS 12:27

GOD of rich and poor alike, help me to be content with what I have. Help me to think before I accumulate. Help me to be a distributor rather than a hoarder.

Being kidnapped
and held for ransom
never worries the poor.

PROVERBS 13:8

JUDGE OF ALL
people, our
nature is tainted,
and we lack
discernment.
I am depending
on you
to help me tell
the dead ends
from your perfect
path. Help me
not to shrink
from the right
choice, however
painful or
unpopular.

Before each and every person there lies a wide and pleasant road that seems right but ends in death

PROVERBS 14:12

ROCK of the
Ages, thank you
for strength
beyond
the health club.
Thank you
for family
security that
exceeds police
protection.

REVERENCE FOR GOD

HIS CHILDREN HAVE A PLACE OF REFUGE AND SECURITY

GIVES A MAN DEEP STRENGTH

PROVERBS 14:26

PRINCE of Peace, help me to exercise self-control the next time things don't go my way. Help me to see the surprising power in gentleness.

A gentle answer turns away wrath but harsh words cause quarrels quarrels quarrels quarrels

PROVERBS 15:1

*MASTER of the
Universe, purify
my attitudes.
Help me to love
the people with
whom I have
influence. And
help me never to
lose the wonder
of learning.*

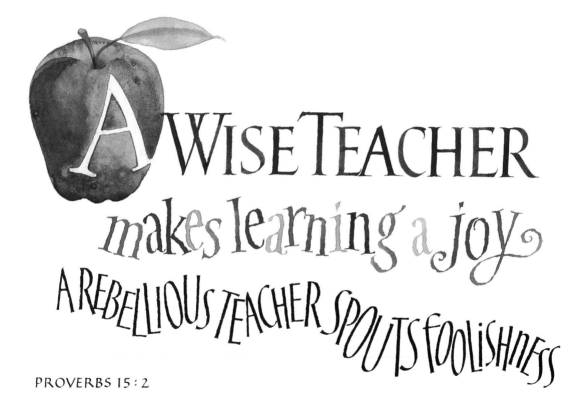

A WISE TEACHER makes learning a joy A REBELLIOUS TEACHER SPOUTS foolishness

PROVERBS 15:2

TO GOD,
who is my friend,
thank you for
the beauty of
simplicity and
the value of
love between
two people.
Help me
cultivate
that love.

It is better to eat soup with someone you love than steak with someone you hate.

PROVERBS 15:17

THANK YOU, Lord, for friends who are honest enough to point out my blind spots. Give me the courage to follow through.

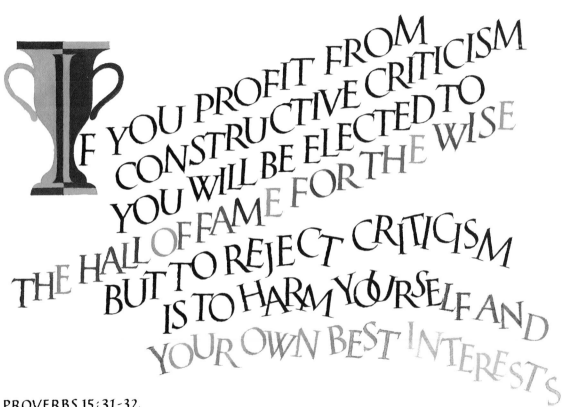

IF YOU PROFIT FROM CONSTRUCTIVE CRITICISM YOU WILL BE ELECTED TO THE HALL OF FAME FOR THE WISE BUT TO REJECT CRITICISM IS TO HARM YOURSELF AND YOUR OWN BEST INTERESTS

PROVERBS 15:31-32

SOVEREIGN God,
how limited is
my perspective
compared to your
omniscience
and boundless
creativity!
Thank you for
being my partner
in the journey.
With this
knowledge
I can go about
life confidently.

A little gained honestly
is better than
GREAT WEALTH
gotten by dishonest means

THE LORD DEMANDS FAIRNESS IN EVERY BUSINESS DEAL

PROVERBS 16:8,11

LORD
and Master,
I see that
pride is very
dangerous.
I acknowledge
my gift to be
from you.
I also recognize
the importance
of my family
and mentors
in nurturing
me along
the way.

PRIDE GOES BEFORE DESTRUCTION AND HAUGHTINESS BEFORE A FALL

PROVERBS 16:18

LORD of industry, thank you for the work I have to do. Help me to see the blessing in busyness.

Idle hands are the devil's workshop idle lips are his mouthpiece

PROVERBS 16:27

*GOD
of our fathers,
thank you for the
white-haired
people
in my life.
Teach me what it
means to be godly.*

White hair is a crown of glory and is seen most among the godly.

PROVERBS 16:31

*HEAVENLY
Father, in your
best time,
may we bring
joy to our
grandparents,
present children
to our parents,
and live to see
our own
grandchildren.*

AN OLD MAN's grandchildren are his crowning glory

PROVERBS 17:6

*LORD, you are
the joy-giver!
Thank you for
the merry sounds
of singing birds,
ringing bells,
and whistling
workers.
Help me to
spread joy all
around me.*

A cheerful heart
does good like medicine
but a broken spirit makes one sick

PROVERBS 17:22

ALMIGHTY God,
I am not
ashamed to
admit my need
of you.
I am protected
when I stick
with you.
There really is
safety in this
world today.
Hallelujah!

THE LORD

is a strong fortress

The godly run to him and are safe

PROVERBS 18:10

CREATOR God,
thank you for all
the possibilities
that exist and the
freedom to
explore them.
Help me to be
open-minded,
always testing,
ever curious.

INTELLIGENT PEOPLE ARE ALWAYS OPEN TO new ideas

IN FACT THEY LOOK FOR THEM

LOOK FOR THEM

PROVERBS 18:15

LORD of Truth,
help me not
to be fooled
by feelings.
Teach me to
be objective.
Help me
not to jump to
conclusions until
all the facts are
known.

Any story sounds true until someone tells the other side and sets the record straight.

PROVERBS 18:17

GOD, who is love, forgive us for the enmity that has developed between the sexes. Help us to find the fulfillment that exists in giving ourselves freely to each other.

THE MAN who finds a wife
finds a good thing
She is a blessing to him from the LORD

PROVERBS 18:22

DEAR GOD,
you alone are the
perfect friend.
Help me to
hold up my end
of friendships
and take the time
just to hang out,
even when it's not
convenient.

HERE are "friends" who
pretend to be friends,
but there is a friend
who sticks closer than a brother

PROVERBS 18:24

LORD of my family, thank you for an honest father. What a responsibility! Help me to realize that the decisions I make today will affect the next generation.

'Tis a wonderful heritage to have an Honest Father

PROVERBS 20:7

OUR FATHER,
help us to value
and recognize the
significance of
the children
around us.
Help us to
take seriously
our training
of children
from their
earliest days.

THE CHARACTER of
even a child can be known
by the way he acts.

PROVERBS 20:11

LORD GOD,
I confess
that my wisdom
is so limited
compared to yours.
Help me to
relax!

SINCE THE LORD
IS DIRECTING OUR STEPS
Why try to understand
everything that happens
along the way?

PROVERBS 20:24

RIGHTEOUS
God, forgive us
for romanticizing
crime. Help us to
recapture the
seriousness of
breaking
the law.

WISE KING
stamps out crime by severe punishment.

PROVERBS 20:26

LORD of the ages, forgive us for allowing the generations to become polarized. Help us to respect each other's preferences and not miss out on what we have to give to each other.

The glory of young men is their strength;

of old men, their experience.

PROVERBS 20:29

MASTER of all peoples, I don't know how you can be in control of hundreds of governments at the same time, but I'm glad that you are!

Just as water's turned into irrigation ditches so the Lord directs the king's thoughts

PROVERBS 21:1

I PRAISE YOU,
God, for being on
the side of justice.
Help me
remember that
other people need
my gifts more
than you do.

GOD is more pleased when we are just and fair than when we give him gifts

PROVERBS 21:3

DEAR LORD,
how precious is
peace. Help me to
contribute in
spirit to making
our home
beautiful inside
and out.

IT IS BETTER to live in the corner of an attic than with a crabby woman in a lovely home

PROVERBS 21:9

*GOD of
compassion,
I thank you
that there is
justice
in the universe.
Forgive me
for insulating
myself from the
disadvantaged.
Soften
my heart.*

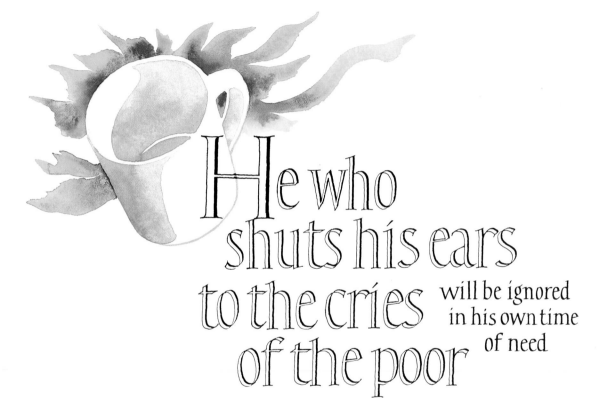

He who
shuts his ears
to the cries   will be ignored
of the poor   in his own time
of need

PROVERBS 21:13

LORD of history, thank you for the sacrifice of my family in the past to give me the privileges I enjoy today. Help me to care about the next generation.

WISE PEOPLE
save for the future
but the foolish spend whatever they get
spend whatever they get
whatever they get

PROVERBS 21:20

LORD GOD,
whose name is
above all names,
help me to reflect
your character
and excellence.
Help me to
develop
long-term
relationships
through
dependable
work.

F you must choose, take A GOOD NAME *rather than Great Riches. For to be held in loving esteem is better than silver and gold.*

PROVERBS 22:1

*MASTER, help us
to realize our
responsibility!
We need your
wisdom so that
we will teach
your way and not
some caricature
of it.*

Teach a child to choose the right path and when he is older he will remain upon it

PROVERBS 22:6

HOLY GOD,
give us the
discernment
to deal fairly
with dissenters.
Give us
the courage to
stand against
destructive forces.

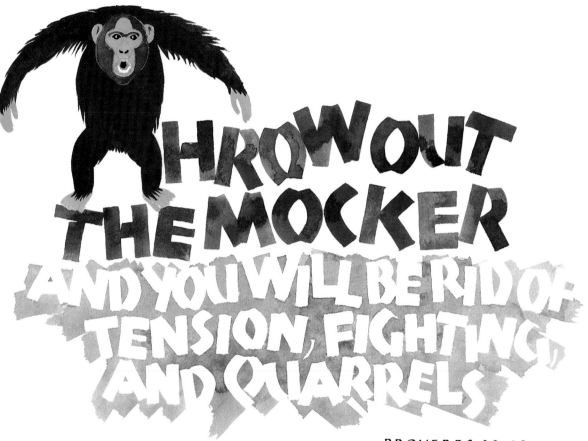

THROW OUT THE MOCKER AND YOU WILL BE RID OF TENSION, FIGHTING, AND QUARRELS

PROVERBS 22:10

LORD and Master, help us to take seriously the universal defiance of human nature. Help us to act with authority, but in such a way that young people will know that it is for their sake.

A youngster's HEART is FILLED with ReBELlion BUT PUNISHment will DRIVE it out of him

PROVERBS 22:15

*GOD of history,
we confess our
greed. Help us to
be content with
what we have
and to champion
the oppressed.*

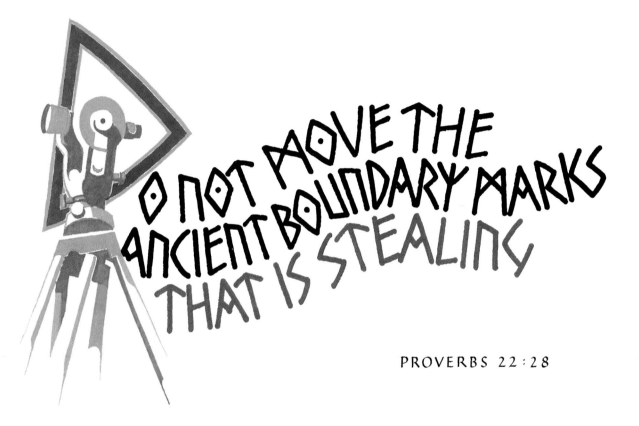

DO NOT MOVE THE ANCIENT BOUNDARY MARKS THAT IS STEALING

PROVERBS 22:28

LORD and Rescuer of our souls, thank you for warning us that drunkenness can lead to disaster. Help us to know when to say no.

DON'T let the sparkle and the smooth taste of strong wine deceive you. For in the end it bites like a poisonous serpent. PROVERBS 23:31-32

MASTER
of our minds,
help me to make
the time to plan.
Help me think
things through
before I act.
Help me to keep
learning.

Any enterprise
IS BUILT BY WISE PLANNING
BECOMES STRONG
THROUGH COMMON SENSE
AND PROFITS WONDERFULLY
BY KEEPING ABREAST
OF THE FACTS

PROVERBS 24:3-4

*LORD
of all fairness,
help me to
recognize both
your judgment
and your
grace.*

Do not rejoice
when your
enemy meets trouble.
Let there be no gladness
when he falls.

PROVERBS 24:17

*LORD of perfect
knowledge,
help me to
remember that
you are God.
Thank you for
keeping from me
what is best
for me
not to know.*

IT IS GOD's PRIVILEGE to conceal things

PROVERBS 25:2

GREAT Counselor, help me to develop the sensitivity to know when to give advice. Help me not to hold back words that could be crucial to another person's future.

TIMELY ADVICE

is as lovely as gold apples

in a silver basket

PROVERBS 25:11

*LORD OF ALL
who work, help
me to do my part
to make the
business
successful.
Help me not to
add to the stress
management
bears, but to
remember that
they, also,
are accountable
to you.*

A faithful employee is as refreshing as a cool day in the hot summertime

PROVERBS 25:13

*PATIENT Lord,
thank you for the
experience of age
that bears out
this truth. Keep
my own bones
soft.*

BE PATIENT AND YOU WILL FINALLY WIN for a soft tongue can break hard bones

PROVERBS 25:15

GOD of Truth,
help me to
remember the
severe damage
that results from
not speaking
truthfully.

TELLING LIES about someone is as harmful as hitting him with an axe.

PROVERBS 25:18

LORD, thank you for those in my life who aren't satisfied with me. Help me to learn from the pain. Give me the courage to be this kind of friend.

Wounds from a friend
ARE BETTER THAN
kisses from an enemy.

PROVERBS 27:6

TO THE GOD
who freely gives,
help me not to be
so stingy.

A WORKER MAY EAT FROM THE ORCHARD HE TENDS

Anyone should be rewarded who protects another's interests

PROVERBS 27:18

LORD of reality,
you see behind
our masks.
Forgive us
for our polite
dishonesty.
Help me to be
genuine through
and through.

MIRROR
REFLECTS A
PERSON'S FACE

BUT WHAT HE IS REALLY LIKE
IS SHOWN BY THE KIND OF
FRIENDS HE CHOOSES

PROVERBS 27:19

SPIRIT of God,
keep me from
being spoiled by
others' praise.
Help me to
remember that
your opinion
matters most.

The purity of silver and gold can be tested in a crucible but people are tested by their reaction to praise

PROVERBS 27:21

HOLY GOD,
we confess that
we have strayed
from your path.
Please guide our
leaders. Help
them to live
uprightly. Help
us get back on
track.

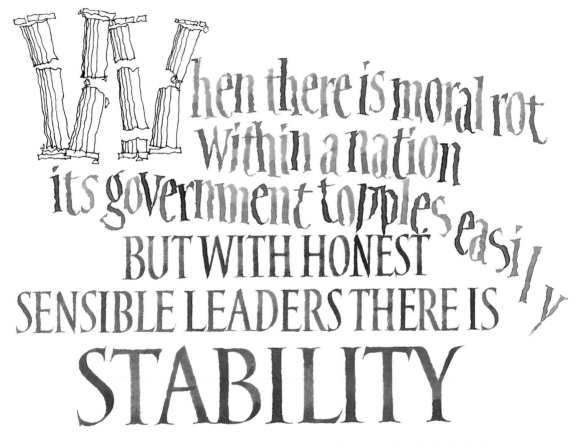

When there is moral rot within a nation its government topples easily BUT WITH HONEST SENSIBLE LEADERS THERE IS STABILITY

PROVERBS 28:2

GOD of grace,
forgive me
for being
stiff-necked.
Help me to
learn from
my mistakes.

EOPLE who refuse to admit their mistakes can never be successful. But if they confess and forsake them, they get another chance.

PROVERBS 28:13

*LORD of
equality, help us
to view each
other the way
you see us. Thank you for
sustaining the
universe.*

Rich and poor are alike in this: each depends on God for light

PROVERBS 29:13

LORD GOD,
we need your
final authority
to keep us from
destroying
ourselves.
Help us
to realize that
joy follows
obedience.
Thank you for
those who teach
your words
of life.

Where there is
ignorance of God
crime runs wild

but what a wonderful thing it is
for a nation to know and keep
HIS LAWS

PROVERBS 29:18

*AUTHOR of
Truth, help us to
become more
familiar with
your revelation.
Thank you for
centuries of
testing that bear
its truthfulness.
Thank you for
experiences in my
own life that
authenticate your
wisdom.*

PROVERBS 30:5

EVERY Word of GOD PROVES TRUE

*LORD
of creation,
thank you for
making women!
And thank you
for the deeper
beauty of
character that
outlasts physical
appearance.*

CHARM can be deceptive
and beauty doesn't last,
but a woman who fears
and reverences God
shall be greatly praised

PROVERBS 31:30

*Topical
Index
to the
Proverbs
in This
Book*

. . .